RUDY
AND THE
FORBIDDEN LAKE

WRITTEN BY
PAUL WESTMORELAND

PICTURES BY
GEORGE ERMOS

OXFORD
UNIVERSITY PRESS

A CHILDREN'S

RUDY

AND THE

FORBIDDEN
LAKE

This book is dedicated to Finn, Charlie, and Maggie. — P.W.

Dedicated to Zina, thanks for your support and enthusiasm! — G.E.

OXFORD
UNIVERSITY PRESS

Great Clarendon Street, Oxford OX2 6DP
Oxford University Press is a department of the University of Oxford.
It furthers the University's objective of excellence in research, scholarship,
and education by publishing worldwide. Oxford is a registered trade mark
of Oxford University Press in the UK and in certain other countries

Text copyright © Paul Westmoreland 2023
Illustrations copyright © George Ermos 2023

The moral rights of the author have been asserted

Database right Oxford University Press (maker)

First published in 2023

British Library Cataloguing in Publication Data

Data available

ISBN: 978-0-19-278257-1

1 3 5 7 9 10 8 6 4 2

Printed in China

Paper used in the production of this book is a natural,
recyclable product made from wood grown in sustainable forests.
The manufacturing process conforms to the environmental
regulations of the country of origin.

ST RIGAMORE'S
ACADEMY

THE SKATEWAY

MAPLESTONE PARK

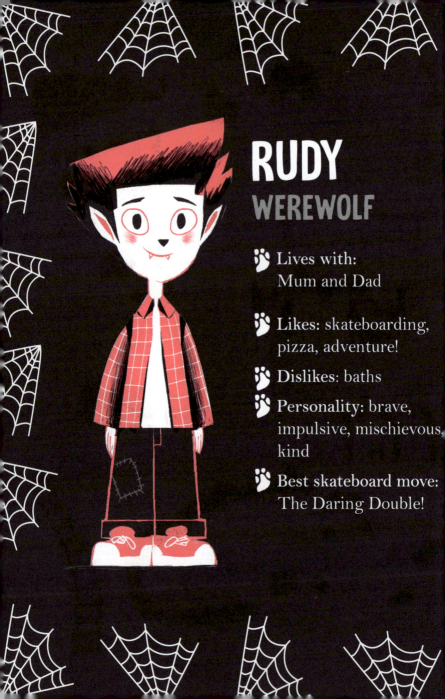

RUDY
WEREWOLF

🐾 Lives with:
Mum and Dad

🐾 Likes: skateboarding,
pizza, adventure!

🐾 Dislikes: baths

🐾 Personality: brave,
impulsive, mischievous,
kind

🐾 Best skateboard move:
The Daring Double!

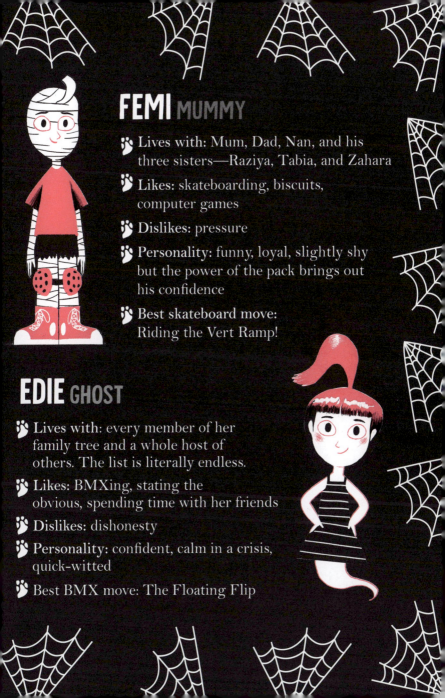

FEMI MUMMY

- Lives with: Mum, Dad, Nan, and his three sisters—Raziya, Tabia, and Zahara
- Likes: skateboarding, biscuits, computer games
- Dislikes: pressure
- Personality: funny, loyal, slightly shy but the power of the pack brings out his confidence
- Best skateboard move: Riding the Vert Ramp!

EDIE GHOST

- Lives with: every member of her family tree and a whole host of others. The list is literally endless.
- Likes: BMXing, stating the obvious, spending time with her friends
- Dislikes: dishonesty
- Personality: confident, calm in a crisis, quick-witted
- Best BMX move: The Floating Flip

CHAPTER
ONE

It was the very depths of winter. The days were drawing so short, the sky above the church that overlooked the town square was darkening, and Rudy and his two best friends, Edie and Femi, were only just finishing their lunch. Here in Cobble Cross, the shorter days always stirred up excitement. The winter solstice was the high point of the season and the celebrations were just one day away.

The Kindheart Community Hall was buzzing with excitement as everyone pitched in to prepare for the party. Rudy's school friends were there, along with his vampiric teacher, Mr Hunter. Even Mr Ding, the bat-faced bus driver, and Ms Gunther, the troll-lady from the school canteen, were lending a hand.

'Here you go, Rudy,' his mum said, passing him a dusty box. 'Take this and help

Jackie O'Lantern. She's in charge of putting up the bunting.' Mum pointed across the hall to an orange-faced woman positioning a stepladder by the stage. She had a huge smile and her eyes shone with a warm glow.

'No problem!' Rudy smiled, and Wolfie, his beloved cub, pawed a loose string hanging from the box.

'Edie, can you help the Skeleton Ska Band test their microphones?' Rudy's mum asked.

'Sure!' Edie smiled.

'And Femi, can you go and untangle the fairy lights, please?'

'Absolutely!' Femi saluted with a flap of his loose bandages. 'I'm good at untangling things.'

'Thank you.' Rudy's mum smiled. Then she noticed something. 'Hey! What do you think you're doing?'

Rudy's dad looked up from a plate of sandwiches he was scoffing, and a guilty smile stretched across his face.

'Put those back!' Mum said. 'They're for everyone to share!'

Dad's face began to burn with embarrassment. 'But I only took one . . . plate.'

'Just because you like the look of something, it doesn't mean you can help yourself to it!' Mum said. 'Now go and organize the midnight fireworks!'

'Sorry.' Dad swallowed his last bite and put the sandwiches back on the refreshments table.

'I can't believe we're finally allowed to stay up for the fireworks,' Rudy said as the three friends wandered across the hall to start their jobs.

Femi nodded. 'It's going to be awesome.'

'Yeah. I usually watch them from my bedroom,' Edie said with a sneaky smile.

Rudy and Femi gasped with jealousy.

'Staying up is a perk of being a ghost,' Edie said with a shrug.

Jackie O'Lantern's smile beamed as Rudy arrived with the box of bunting. 'Perfect timing,' she said.

Rudy watched as Jackie opened her toolbox. Layer upon layer of trays slid apart like a magic trick, each one filled with all kinds of tools Rudy had never seen before. There were pliers and spanners you could tighten, clips and clamps, all kinds of saws— some that cut pipes, some that cut holes.

There was even a hammer with Jackie's name engraved on it.

'Wow! Are you a superhero?' Rudy asked as Jackie fastened a toolbelt around her waist.

'No, I just like fixing things folks can't repair for themselves.' Jackie smiled.

Rudy was very impressed. 'The only tools in our house are a box of screwdrivers and a rusty old saw.'

'Well, I've spent a long time collecting these, and I can't do my job without them,' Jackie said. 'Come on, we've got work to do!'

Jackie climbed the stepladder, and Rudy began passing her the bunting.

In no time, the hall was ready. The fairy lights were twinkling. The Skeleton Ska Band were sounding great. The bunting was up and a banner declared:

The sky grew even darker as Ms Gunther locked up and everyone set off for home. Heavy, ominous clouds were rolling in, blotting out the stars and the moon. Wolfie whined as a fat raindrop splattered on his nose.

'It's all right,' Rudy said, picking him up. 'We'll be home soon.'

The rain grew heavier as Rudy, his parents, and his friends hurried along the streets. When they reached the junction at the end of Femi's road, thunder rumbled in the distance. 'See you tomorrow,' Rudy called out, and they all ran the last bit home.

Rudy made it back just as the clouds burst. It rained so hard, the drops were

bouncing up off the ground and
splashing down again!

As Rudy dried off, a mighty crash of
thunder blasted out of the sky—

KA-BOOOOOOMM!

The whole house shook as though the
town was being hit by an earthquake, and
Wolfie bolted under Rudy's bed.

Rudy couldn't blame him. In fact, it gave
him an idea!

As the storm set in, Rudy pulled the
sheet off his bed and tied it between his
drawers and the wardrobe, the same way
Jackie had hung the bunting in Kindheart
Hall. In no time, he'd made a den that would

keep them both safe from the thunder all night.

Rudy laid his pillow and duvet inside the den, but just as he snuggled down with Wolfie, the whole house was plunged into darkness! The only light was the occasional flash of lightning from the raging storm outside.

Rudy gave the cub a reassuring cuddle. 'Don't worry, Wolfie, it's only a power cut.'

As the rain peppered the window like handfuls of gravel being flung in a fit of rage, something went—

CRREEEAAKK!

Rudy peered out of the den. A strange flickering light was creeping around the door. He frowned, focusing his eyes, and realized the light was from Dad's old silver candlestick.

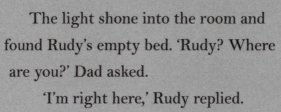

The light shone into the room and found Rudy's empty bed. 'Rudy? Where are you?' Dad asked.

'I'm right here,' Rudy replied.

The light swept across the room and found the den. 'Ah!' Dad said. 'Good thinking!'

Rudy smiled, and Wolfie replied with a happy yap!

'It's a bad storm,' Dad said. 'I'll check the fuse box, but there might not be power until the morning. Just hunker down for the night and sleep as best you can, OK?'

'Sure, Dad. We'll be fine,' Rudy said.

'Night,' Dad said, and shut the door.

Rudy and Wolfie snuggled down and tried to sleep, but the storm kept them awake for hours. It wasn't just the rain and thunder going—

PITTER-PATTER—KA-BOOOMM!

Rudy could also hear the branches of trees going—

KERR-SNAAPP!

And roof tiles slipping off—

SMMMERSSHH!

Eventually, Rudy drifted off, imagining all the damage they'd find in the morning . . .

CHAPTER TWO

When Rudy woke up in the morning, the storm had passed. The sky was clear, and it looked like a bright winter's day.

Rudy's tummy rumbled as he and Wolfie padded downstairs for breakfast. Mum was on the phone, looking worried, while Dad was rummaging through the kitchen drawers. 'Morning, son,' he said. 'Have you seen my silver candlestick?'

'No, sorry,' Rudy replied.

Dad made a frustrated sigh and started yanking open the cupboards.

As Rudy filled Wolfie's bowl and poured himself some cereal, Mum put down the phone. The colour had drained from her face. 'I've got some bad news,' she said, sitting down.

Rudy stared at her across the kitchen table. As hungry as he was, this seemed important, so food would have to wait.

'The storm has left an awful mess,' Mum said.

'Oh no,' Rudy gasped.

'Do you think my candlestick blew away?' Dad asked.

'Stranger things have happened,' Mum replied, rolling her eyes.

Rudy could tell this was just a silly answer to Dad's silly question, but Dad looked over from the cupboard with a serious look.

'I doubt it's gone far,' Mum said, sounding serious. 'But all sorts of things have been blown around town. Some people have lost a lot more than just a candlestick!

'The railway line is blocked with football nets. The Slime Fried Chicken sign flew all the way to Colonel Sanderson's farm, and there's a bus stop on the school field! Mr Ding is lucky that someone reported it because his glasses have gone too. He's as blind as a . . . *well*. He can't look for anything until he finds them.'

'Is that it?' Dad shook his head and continued his search.

'No it isn't, *Graham*!' Mum snorted. 'There was so much rain, the pond in Maplestone Park flooded and turned half the roads into rivers!'

Rudy's jaw dropped. He'd never heard of anything like this happening in Cobble Cross before.

'It's a nightmare.' Mum sighed and poured herself a comforting cup of tea.

'Don't worry.' Rudy smiled. 'We still have

the solstice celebrations to look forward to.'

Mum looked up from her tea. 'Oh, I doubt that. The storm blew the roof off Kindheart Hall.'

Rudy was so shocked he dropped his spoon and cereal splashed across the table. 'There must be something we can do?' he said.

'I wish there was,' Mum replied. 'But ven if the whole town pitches in to help, I doubt we'll fix everything in time. It's a shame, but I expect the party's cancelled.'

Rudy sighed. He felt so disappointed, he lost his appetite.

To cheer himself up, Rudy grabbed his skateboard and set off to meet his friends at the Skateway.

Every street, yard, and garden Rudy
skated past was a soggy mess. The rain had
left streams trickling along the gutters, and
some gardens were flooded like ponds.

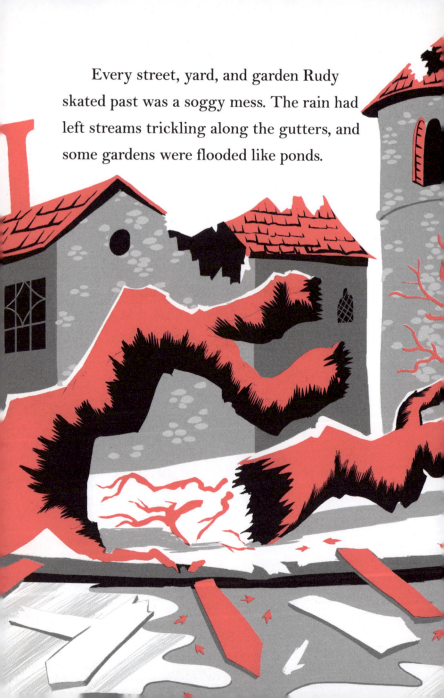

The wind had uprooted entire trees and left them lying across roads and roundabouts. A few had even karate-chopped through cars. It was as though the weather had had a full-on temper tantrum!

'That storm was brutal,' Rudy said, as he met Femi and Edie.

'Yeah!' Femi nodded. 'It left a canoe in our apple tree!'

'I heard all the hairdryers from Rita's Salon blew away,' Edie said.

'Wow,' Rudy said, amazed. 'We must've been lucky. My dad only lost his silver candlestick.'

'That's funny,' Femi said, staring at Rudy. 'My parents lost a silver platter they were going to use for the buffet. The plates were fine though.'

'That is odd,' Edie said with an intrigued frown.

'We should go to Kindheart Hall. Maybe we can help everyone clean up?' Rudy suggested.

Femi and Edie agreed, and they all
set off.

When they arrived, Rudy's jaw dropped.
Roof tiles were lying strewn across the
square, as though an enormous monster had
peeled the roof off Kindheart Hall like it
was opening a can of sardines! The bunting
he'd helped Jackie put up was still hanging
though, only now it looked like a bedraggled
washing line that had been left out in
the rain.

Rudy and his friends stared at the
wreckage, while helpers began sweeping up
the shattered slates and splintered joists.

Jackie O'Lantern was there too, but to
Rudy's surprise, she wasn't hard at work.
Instead, she looked dejected as she swept up
some leaves blown in by the storm.

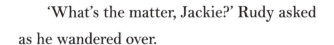

'What's the matter, Jackie?' Rudy asked as he wandered over.

'There's so much to fix, but I can't do anything,' Jackie said, sounding dismal. 'My entire toolbox vanished in the storm. All my tools—gone!' The warm glow in her eyes had almost disappeared too. 'I can't fix the roof or help much without them.'

'Oh, I'm sorry,' Rudy said.

'That's odd,' Edie said, and her intrigued frown returned.

'I know,' Femi said. 'Jackie, if we can find your toolbox, could you fix the roof and save the solstice celebrations?'

Rudy's ears pricked up.

A glimmer of Jackie's smile returned. 'I'd love to, but I'm not sure that'd be enough. All the decorations are ruined, and the Skeleton Ska Band have lost their trumpet!'

'It wouldn't be much of a party without decorations and music!' Edie agreed.

'Yeah, but we have to try,' Rudy said. 'The winters in Cobble Cross are so long and dark, the solstice celebrations are the one thing most folks look forward to.'

'It's a nice thought, guys,' Jackie said. 'But if we can't repair the roof, Kindheart

Hall will probably be condemned.'

Rudy gasped.

'I am sorry,' Jackie said with a sad smile, and went back to sweeping up the leaves.

'Golly,' Edie said. 'If they tear down the hall, there'll be no more solstice celebrations—*ever*!'

'That'd be an even bigger disaster than the storm,' Femi said.

'Yes it would,' Rudy said, his face filling with determination. 'But if we find Jackie's toolbox, she can start fixing things and there's a chance we can save the celebrations!'

'That would also keep the tradition alive!' Femi nodded excitedly.

'Yeah, but the whole town's a mess,' Edie said.

'Jackie's toolbox could be anywhere. Does "needle in a haystack" sound familiar?'

'It's OK, I have an idea.' Rudy smiled. 'My mum said the storm flooded the pond in Maplestone Park and turned half the roads into rivers. If Jackie's toolbox was washed away by the rain, there's only one place in Cobble Cross it could have ended up.'

The three friends stared at each other and they all whispered, *'Dankpool Lake in Gnarlybark Forest!'*

'We can't go there!' Femi exclaimed. 'It's forbidden!'

'He's right, Rudy.' Edie nodded. 'You must've heard all the rumours about mysterious bubbling noises and strange goings on. Not to mention all the *disappearances*!'

'Oh, they're just rumours,' Rudy said. 'No one knows if they're actually true.'

'Only because the water's so dark no one's actually seen what's lurking in there,' Femi said with a shiver.

'Oh, come on. We can't give up on the solstice celebrations,' Rudy said. 'We have to at least look.'

'Yeah, OK,' Edie said, struggling to hide her misgivings.

'We're just going to take a quick look, right?' Femi asked.

Rudy nodded. 'And save the solstice celebrations!'

CHAPTER THREE

Streams carrying leaves like boats trickled along every gutter in Cobble Cross. Sure enough, the running water led Rudy and his friends all the way to Gnarlybark Forest. Even though its twisted trees were packed tighter than the school bus on a rainy Monday morning, the storm had whipped through the forest with a vengeance. The chunky, contorted trunks had been ripped up and felled, leaving severed stumps and mounds of sprawling roots blocking the winding pathways.

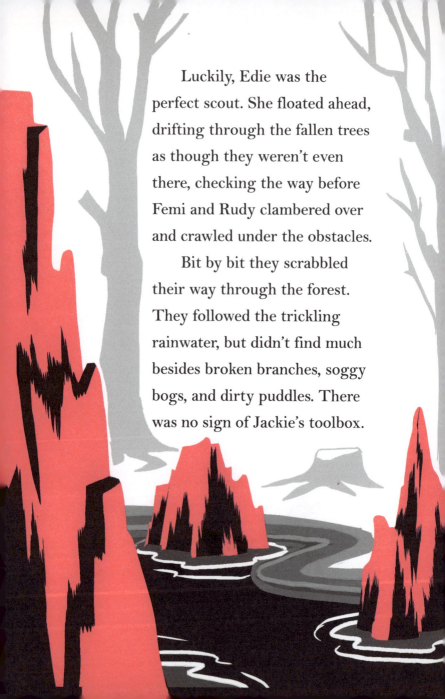

Luckily, Edie was the perfect scout. She floated ahead, drifting through the fallen trees as though they weren't even there, checking the way before Femi and Rudy clambered over and crawled under the obstacles.

Bit by bit they scrabbled their way through the forest. They followed the trickling rainwater, but didn't find much besides broken branches, soggy bogs, and dirty puddles. There was no sign of Jackie's toolbox.

The afternoon wore on until the trees finally parted, revealing the murky shore of Dankpool Lake. It got its name because the surrounding rocky hills were so steep they cut out the dwindling light, and the water was so dark it looked like an enormous puddle of jet-black ink.

Edie floated out over the gloomy lake and stared down into it.

'Can you see anything?' Rudy asked as he and Femi leaned their skateboards against an old tree stump and wandered over to the water's edge.

Edie peered in and shook her head. 'It's too dark.'

Rudy deflated with disappointment.

'Sorry,' Edie said. 'This was a good idea, Rudy, but I think we've had a wasted trip.'

Femi put his hand on Rudy's shoulder. 'Sorry, mate. Let's just go back.'

Rudy scowled into the water. He'd felt certain the rain would've washed all the missing stuff here, but he couldn't deny the fact they hadn't found a single thing.

Rudy grabbed a rock and was about to throw it at the lake in frustration when a voice cried out.

'ARRGGHH!'

Rudy looked around, searching the
trees. But the light was fading as the wintry
evening crept up on him, and he struggled to
see anything.

'There!' Femi said, pointing along
the shore to a distant glowing light. They
hurried over and found the ghost of a gnarly
old, crabby hermit at the foot of a great oak.

'Are you OK?' Edie asked.

The old hermit looked up, his ghostly
face glaring with fury. 'Someone just threw a
stone at me. Was it you?' he
demanded.

'No,' Edie replied,
and Femi and Rudy
shook their heads.

'Liars!' The hermit pointed a claw at the rock in Rudy's hand. 'Just leave me alone will you!' Then he turned with an angry gust and floated away through the darkened trees.

'That was odd,' Edie said.

'It wasn't me, honest,' Rudy said, dropping the rock.

'We know that!' Femi said. 'But who *did* throw it?'

'It doesn't matter,' Edie said, looking around. 'It's getting dark. If we don't get going we might not find our way home.'

'And if the rumours are true, we could disappear!' Femi added.

'Good point.' Rudy nodded.

They were about to set off when Femi stopped in his tracks. 'Hey! Who's taken my skateboard?'

Rudy and Edie looked round.

'I put it right here next to yours,' Femi said, pointing to Rudy's Pitbull-360. 'But it's gone!'

'It must be here somewhere,' Edie said.

'Yeah, come on. Let's look,' Rudy added.

Femi and Edie began searching the trees. As Rudy looked along the shoreline, he heard a—

POP!

The sound made him turn and stare. The lake's dark, ominous waters were as still as a sheet of glass, but Rudy couldn't deny what he'd heard.

Then there was another—

POP!

Rudy's eyes darted this way and that, skimming the lake like stones until he saw a rippling ring spreading out and ebbing away.

Rudy squinted in the dwindling light and, there! Another bubble slipped through the surface, lingered and went—

POP!

Rudy gasped.

Whatever was down there, it was breathing. And that meant only one thing: it was alive!

'Hey!' Rudy shouted.

'Have you found it?' Femi asked.

'No. It's something else,' Rudy said.

Without taking his eyes off the dispersing ripples, Rudy reached down. His fingers walked across the wet shingle until they found a chocolate-coloured pebble. Rudy picked it up, took aim at the ripples and threw it—

PLOOP!

The pebble was on target, and Rudy scored a bullseye right in the centre of the widening rings.

'Yessss!' Rudy punched the air. But the moment he lowered his fist, the same chocolate-coloured pebble shot out of the water, straight back at him!

Rudy ducked before it hit him square in the face. The pebble landed on the shingle with a rattling—

KA-KA-LACK!

Rudy looked up nervously. 'Oops!'

'Not cool, Rudy,' Femi said, frowning.

'Yeah! Let's upset whatever's hiding in Dankpool Lake. That'll get Femi's skateboard back!' Edie's voice rang with sarcasm.

Before Rudy could apologize, the surface of the lake began to boil! Hundreds upon thousands of ferocious bubbles began bursting through the water. There were so

many, they splashed and spat, spraying Rudy
and his friends.

As they stepped back, a large, rubbery
black dome broke through the bubbling
surface and began to rise up.

'ARRRRGGHH!'

Whatever it was, it made all three of them scream and start sprinting for safety among the dense trees. All thoughts of Femi's skateboard and saving the solstice celebrations vanished as they fled. Rudy's feet pounded the ground and his heart thumped in his chest like a war drum!

As they reached the darkened forest, a thought struck Rudy so hard, he stopped.

'Wo-wo-wait!' he called out.

Femi and Edie were already halfway down the wooded pathway, but when they heard their friend, they rushed back.

'What is it?' Edie asked.

'What if that thing took Femi's skateboard?' Rudy asked.

'Then it's welcome to keep it,' Edie said.

Femi gulped and nodded.

'Yeah, but if it did,' Rudy continued, 'it might also have Jackie's toolbox and all the other stuff.'

Edie put her hands on her hips. 'If you want to go and ask it, you're on your own Rudy!'

Femi looked unsure but stood his ground.

'Come on,' Rudy's voice pleaded with his friends. 'Jackie can't fix the roof without her toolbox. If we can get it back, we could save the solstice celebrations, and all future ones. We should at least ask?'

'Yeah, I guess so,' Femi said, wavering.

Edie stayed put. 'Maybe, but no one will mind if we *don't* risk our necks finding out if some monster in Dankpool Lake took a toolbox.'

'Risk our necks?' Rudy frowned. 'It's only thrown a pebble at us. That doesn't make it *dangerous*.'

Femi and Edie stared at Rudy. He could tell they wanted to get out of there, but this was important.

'Who knows,' Rudy said, 'we might even get your skateboard back?'

Femi's feet twisted awkwardly, chewing up the soggy ground. 'OK, let's go and ask it,' he said.

Edie sighed, giving in too. 'On your head be it, wolf boy.'

Rudy smiled and held out his fist. The others gave him a fist bump and they all said,

'*For the power of the pack!*'

CHAPTER FOUR

Rudy, Femi, and Edie cautiously emerged from the twisted trees.

The lake looked as though nothing had happened. The surface was as smooth and dark as a tar pit. The three friends gingerly approached the shoreline. There wasn't so much as a ripple on the water.

Rudy reached down and picked up another pebble.

'Please be careful,' Edie whispered.

'Hey!' Rudy called out and threw the pebble into the lake—

SPLOSH!

The sound echoed off the cliffs as the pebble sank and the ripples faded away. 'Hey!' Rudy cried again. Still nothing.

'Well, we tried.' Femi sighed, sounding relieved. 'Yeah, let's go,' Edie said.

'No, wait,' Rudy said as a tiny bubble rose to the surface and went—

POP!

'It's coming!' Rudy cried, bursting with nervous excitement. 'Oh really?' Femi said, beginning to tremble.

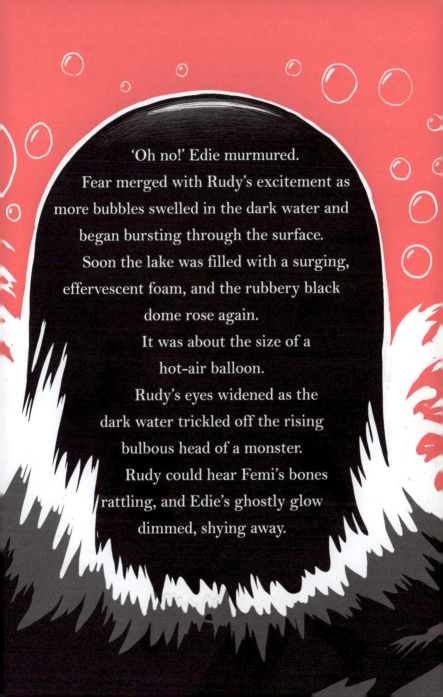

'Oh no!' Edie murmured.

Fear merged with Rudy's excitement as more bubbles swelled in the dark water and began bursting through the surface.

Soon the lake was filled with a surging, effervescent foam, and the rubbery black dome rose again.

It was about the size of a hot-air balloon.

Rudy's eyes widened as the dark water trickled off the rising bulbous head of a monster.

Rudy could hear Femi's bones rattling, and Edie's ghostly glow dimmed, shying away.

The coiled tip of a long, slender tentacle reached out of the water and unfurled, flicking the pebble back at Rudy. This time he was too shocked to duck, and it hit him right between the eyes.

'ARGH!'

As Rudy rubbed his forehead, his friends started yelling! He opened his eyes and to Rudy's horror more long, rubbery tentacles had crept from the lake. One was trying to grab hold of Edie while two more were entangled in Femi's bandages.

Rudy wanted to run but he'd got his friends into this, so he was determined to be brave and get them out of it!

A tentacle twisted in front of Rudy, making the shape of a question mark.

'We know you took my friend's skateboard,' Rudy said. His voice was firm and defiant. 'Did you steal the other things from across town during the storm?'

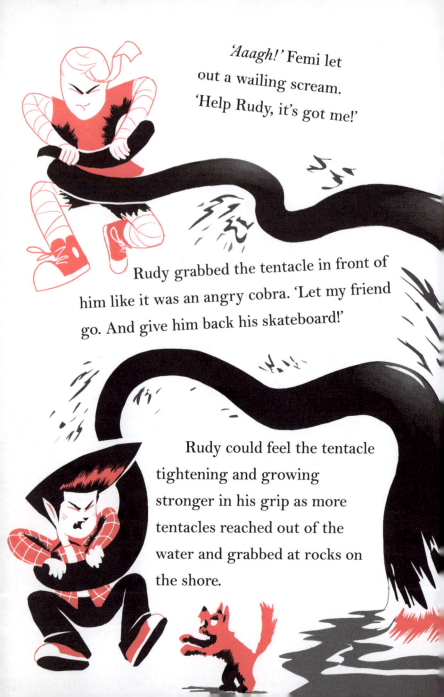

'*Aaagh!*' Femi let out a wailing scream. 'Help Rudy, it's got me!'

Rudy grabbed the tentacle in front of him like it was an angry cobra. 'Let my friend go. And give him back his skateboard!'

Rudy could feel the tentacle tightening and growing stronger in his grip as more tentacles reached out of the water and grabbed at rocks on the shore.

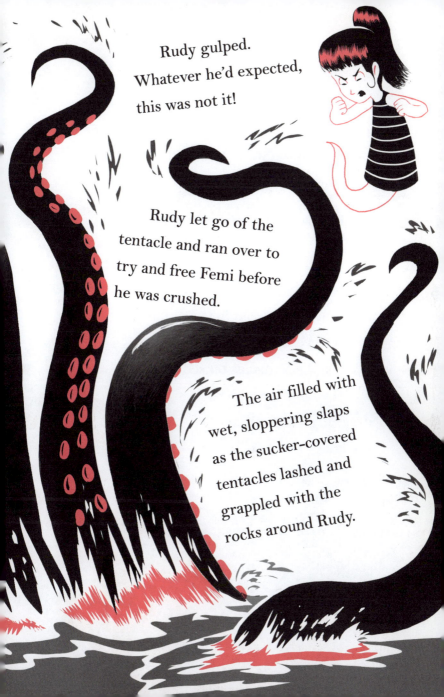

Rudy gulped.
Whatever he'd expected,
this was not it!

Rudy let go of the
tentacle and ran over to
try and free Femi before
he was crushed.

The air filled with
wet, sloppering slaps
as the sucker-covered
tentacles lashed and
grappled with the
rocks around Rudy.

'LET HIM GO!' Rudy shouted, but the
monster wasn't listening. More tentacles
burst from the water, arched like hooks
and dug into the shore. Rudy winced as the
whistling sound of gravel grinding against
rocks bored into his ears like a dentist's drill!

As the tentacles swished around, Edie
waved her hands urging Rudy to start
running, but he couldn't! Femi looked
like his eyeballs might pop out of his
head as the tentacles tensed
and the monster began
dragging itself out of
the lake.

Rudy stared, petrified, as the huge rounded head of a kraken loomed over him. Dribbles of water trickled down it like oil, and large eyelids opened, revealing wide, acid-yellow eyes. The staring eyes narrowed, focusing in on Rudy.

Rudy's legs shook, but he was determined to stand his ground. 'Hey!' he yelled. 'Let go of my friend!'

To everyone's relief, the kraken settled on the shore and let Femi go. 'I only wanted to play with him,' it said.

'That wasn't really playing, though, was it?' Edie replied and the kraken's mouth turned down.

Rudy stared at the mournful-looking monster. He'd half expected its mouth to open wide and swallow him whole, but it didn't seem very dangerous now.

'I'm Rudy and these are my friends, Femi and Edie,' he said, offering the monster a smile. 'What's your name?'

'Squibly,' the kraken replied.

'Did you steal my skateboard?' Femi asked.

Squibly blinked his huge eyes and shook his head. 'No! I haven't stolen anything. I only threw the stone at that old ghost to distract you because I rather liked the look of the slidey-wheely-thing that was lying over there.' Squibly pointed to the tree stump. 'It looked like fun to play with.'

'It *is* fun to play with,' Femi snapped. 'And it's *my* skateboard!'

'Oh!' Squibly slunk back slightly, looking sheepish. 'I didn't think it belonged to anyone—it was just lying around.'

Femi gasped. 'I left it there, but it's still *mine*!'

'Is it?' Squibly frowned.

'Yes, it is,' Edie said. 'So you should give it back, right now!'

Squibly's tentacles tightened around a nearby rock.

Rudy stepped forward. 'I know you like it. It is a lovely slidey-wheely-thing, but it belongs to Femi, and he'd like it back.'

Squibly reluctantly reached a tentacle into the lake. It splashed around a bit, then rose up and dropped the soggy skateboard in front of Femi.

'Thank you.' Femi was very pleased to have it back.

Squibly looked like he was about to sulk back into the lake, but Rudy still had a question that needed answering. 'Have you, by any chance, *picked up* anything else that was lying around?'

'Er . . . *maybe*,' Squibly murmured. 'I lost all my toys when the storm flooded my home, so I decided to replace them. It was fun at first, exploring the town, but the flood got worse, and I was washed away . . . here. I've been quite lonely stuck in this lake. I miss my home so much and having a few nice things really cheered me up. I didn't mean to steal anything.'

'It's understandable,' Edie said. 'But it's wrong to take things that don't belong to you.'

'Yeah,' Rudy nodded. 'Just because you like the look of something, it doesn't mean you can help yourself to it. It makes people sad, the same way you miss your home and your toys.'

'What else did you take?' Femi asked.

Squibly reached his tentacles into the lake and began delving around—

PLUNK!

Squibly dropped something on the shore. 'My shiny looky-thing,' he said.

Rudy and his friends stared at the oval object lying on the shingle.

'That's not a *looky-thing*!' Femi said, picking it up. 'It's my parents' silver platter.'

'Oh,' Squibly said. 'What about my clack-clacks? Do they belong to your parents too?'

'*Clack-clacks?*' Edie frowned.

Squibly began swinging something around like a football rattle—

CLACK-CLACK CLACK-CLACK CLACK-CLACK.

'Stop!' Rudy said. 'They're not a toy. They're Mr Ding's glasses!'

Squibly stopped waving around the clack-clacks and dropped them into Rudy's hands.

'You got anything else stashed away down there?' Edie asked.

Squibly's tentacles began rummaging around in the lake.

'There's my golden tentacle protector,' he said, pulling something else from the lake.

To everyone's horror, Squibly began using it to poke rocks and boulders on the edge of the lake—

'Squibly!' Femi said. 'That's not for protecting your tentacles.'

'Or poking rocks,' Edie added.

'It's a trumpet, and it belongs to the Skeleton Ska Band,' Rudy said.

'It's a what?' Squibly frowned.

'Here, let me show you,' Femi said.

He took the trumpet, pursed his lips, and gave it a blast. A jet of water shot out with a fanfare!

PARRRR!

Squibly plugged his ears with his tentacles.

'We'd better get it back to the skeletons,' Edie said.

Rudy nodded. 'Is that everything you found?'

'I think so,' Squibly replied.

Rudy looked disappointed. 'It's just, we were hoping you had something that belongs to a friend of ours. She needs it to fix the roof of Kindheart Hall or our solstice celebrations will be ruined.'

Squibly thought hard and searched the lake-bed. Gradually an uncomfortable look grew across his face. 'Sorry. All I've got is this treasure chest.'

The three friends
stared as Squibly hauled
the chest out of the water
and dropped it on the
sand—

THONK!

'That's not a treasure chest!' Edie said.

'Look, the hammer's got "Jackie" engraved on it,' Femi added.

Rudy was overjoyed. 'You're right. It's her toolbox! Now we can fix Kindheart Hall!'

'Great!' Femi smiled. 'Let's head back and get started!'

'Wait! Aren't you guys forgetting something?' Edie said and pointed to Squibly, who was looking sorrowful.

'I'm sorry,' Rudy said. 'We have to go, but we can come back and visit if you like?'

That didn't cheer Squibly up.

'I know!' Femi said. 'If we can fix Kindheart Hall, the whole town will come to the solstice celebrations. There's bound to be someone who can help you get home.'

'That's a brilliant idea!' Rudy said.

Squibly started to smile, but it turned into a look of dread. 'Won't everyone be angry with me for taking their things?'

'Not if you apologize.' Rudy smiled. 'Saying sorry fixes things as well as any toolbox when you mean it. And you do. Come on.'

CHAPTER
FIVE

Cobble Cross was under a blanket of
darkness by the time Rudy and his friends
reached the town square, but Kindheart Hall
was still bustling as everyone pitched in to
clear up the mess left by the storm.

'Hey, we've got Jackie's toolbox,' Rudy
called out in triumph, but everyone was too
busy to notice.

Squibly lifted the trumpet to his lips
and blew—

RAARRRRRRR!

Everyone immediately stopped what they were doing and looked up. The sight of Squibly filled them with panic!

Rudy's dad fell off Jackie's stepladder and landed on a pile of rubbish. His mum howled in horror. Mr Hunter took one look at Squibly and vanished in a puff of smoke, taking his mop with him! The Skeleton Ska Band started shaking out of time, rattling in a terrifying rhythm, and Ms Gunther flipped out and flipped over the buffet table.

In two seconds flat, the calm after the storm had turned into total chaos!

'What's going on?' shouted Mr Ding.

'It's a kraken!' yelled Trevor Dactil, the pointy-faced lizard boy from Rudy's class.

'Where?' cried Mr Ding as he looked around, tripped over, and landed face-first in Mr Hunter's bucket of soapsuds—

SPLOT!

Rudy quickly drew a deep breath, tipped his head back and let out a huge—

Everyone froze and stared at him.

'It's all right,' he said. 'I know Squibly looks scary, but he has something he wants to say.'

The crowd held their nerve and listened.

'Er,' Squibly began, sounding rather nervous. 'I didn't know these things belonged to all of you.' Squibly set down the silver platter, the trumpet, Jackie's toolbox, and Mr Ding's glasses. 'I just found them while I was lost and they cheered me up. When Rudy and his friends found me and explained everything, I felt awful, so we brought them back. I'm very sorry. And to make amends, I'd like to help you out.'

Jackie was the first to approach Squibly. 'Thank you, Squibly, that's very kind of you. And thank you, Rudy, Edie, and Femi.' The light in her eyes fizzed as she was reunited with her tools.

Rudy and his friends smiled too.

'What about my silver candlestick?' Rudy's dad called out.

Everyone turned and stared at him.

Squibly's mouth opened but nothing came out.

'You're not still going on about that thing, are you?' Rudy's mum asked. 'You left it outside when you checked the fuse box. Sorry, I thought you knew.'

Dad cringed with embarrassment. 'Oh, never mind then.'

The skeletons took back their trumpet, and Femi's mum picked up her platter. As Mr Ding wiped the soapsuds off his face, Rudy handed him his glasses.

As soon as Mr Ding's eyes focused on Squibly, he panicked again, flew into a flap, and fell into the puddle left by the bucket!

SP-LOOT!

This time, everyone laughed. Even Mr
Ding.

Before long, everyone was hard at work,
pitching in and helping with the repairs.
Rudy and his friends joined in too and Mr
Ding was cleaned up so he could see what he
was doing. But even with the help of Jackie's
toolbox, there was still a lot to do.

As Jackie climbed her stepladder, Squibly slithered over. 'I meant what I said about helping out,' he said.

'That's great, but what can you do?' Jackie asked.

'Anything!' Squibly replied. 'I have eight long arms and they can all do something.'

'Ah!' Jackie said as an idea struck her. 'You *can* help me, then.'

She started calling out instructions, and in no time Squibly was holding up the joists, and Jackie was nailing them back together. When that was done, Rudy and Femi brought Squibly the roof tiles, and he lifted them up so Jackie could pin them into place.

Next, it was painting. Squibly set to work with three brushes and five rollers while Jackie and Rudy hung the rest of the bunting!

They made a dynamite team, and before long Kindheart Hall was ready for a party.

As the last bits of bunting went up, the Skeleton Ska Band started to play. The music carried across the town, and everyone from all over Cobble Cross began arriving with wonderful platters of food, and the solstice celebrations got underway.

'Well done, Squibly,' Rudy said and high-fived a tentacle.

Rudy, Femi, and Edie were the first to hit the dance floor and showed off all their best robot moves. Femi even threw in some bits of break-dancing he'd been practising with his skateboard!

As soon as the covers came off the buffet, Rudy's dad began loading his plate with something from every platter.

The dance floor filled up too, and Squibly let the little kids ride on his tentacles. He lifted them up and down as he twirled around like a merry-go-round.

As each song ended the next one began, and the evening flew by in a haze of laughter and crazy dancing.

At one point, everyone formed a conga and snaked around the hall, kicking and dancing. Squibly even joined the band on stage and borrowed their trumpet, wowing the crowd with a blasting fanfare—

PURRR-PAR-PAR-PA-RRRRRRR!

As everyone burst into a round
of applause, the church clock outside
ticked closer to midnight.

CHAPTER SIX

The bass from the band thumped across the town square as midnight approached, and Rudy headed outside to find a good spot to watch the fireworks. He was tired after all the dancing and it felt good to sit down and gaze up at the moon.

It was full and Rudy couldn't resist it.

He took a deep breath and something went—

SLAP, SLAP, SLOPP!

'Hi!' Squibly said as Rudy looked around. 'What are you doing?'

'I was about to howl at the moon,' Rudy replied. 'It's a werewolf thing.' He tipped his head back and let out a—

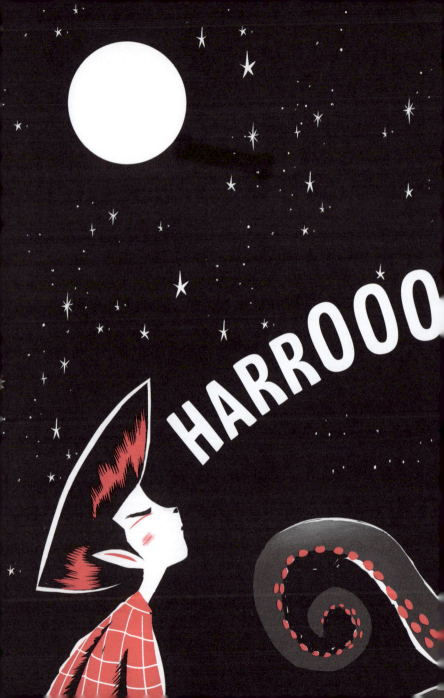

As his howl sailed away, Squibly took a
deep breath and tried to howl—

HA-ROooool!

It started off with the right intentions,
but it quickly fizzled out.

'Never mind,' Rudy reassured him.
'Howling takes practice. I used to have
lessons.'

'I don't need lessons,' Squibly replied, and
Rudy frowned. 'I've got this!'

A tentacle reached round and Squibly
brought the trumpet to his lips—

'That was awesome!' Rudy beamed.

'There you are,' Edie said as she floated over with Femi.

'I thought I'd better bag us a good spot for the fireworks,' Rudy replied.

'Great idea.' Femi smiled and sat beside him.

'Thanks again for bringing me here,' Squibly said. 'If it wasn't for you guys, I'd still be sloshing around in Dankpool Lake.'

'You're welcome,' Rudy replied.

'The solstice celebrations would've been ruined if you hadn't returned Jackie's toolbox,' Edie said.

'And helped us out!' Femi added.

'Well, I've really enjoyed it,' Squibly said. 'But I'd still like to go home.'

'Of course. Where is it?' Rudy asked.

'I don't know,' Squibly replied. 'I got lost when the flood washed me away.'

'What does it look like?' Edie asked.

'Well, there was water—loads of it—but it wasn't dark like Dankpool Lake,' Squibly replied.

'Was it the swimming pool?' Femi suggested.

'No, there were trees all around it,' Squibly said.

'There's a stream in Axemore Woods?' Edie said.

'Does it have rocks and stepping stones?' Squibly asked.

'No. But I know somewhere that does!' Rudy cried as the church bells struck midnight—

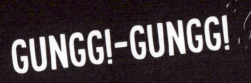

GUNGG!–GUNGG!

Fireworks burst across the sky!

POOMF-
BA-BOOOM!

As everyone crowded into the town square, Cobble Cross filled with chiming bells and whizzing, crackling bangs.

'There's only one place with water, trees, rocks, and stepping stones,' Rudy shouted over the noise. 'The pond in Maplestone Park. That's Squibly's home!'

'Of course!' Edie smiled.

'Awesome!' Femi said.

'Thank you!' Squibly grinned.

'We'll go after the fireworks,' Rudy said and they all sat back to watch.

As more fireworks raced into the sky, something dark and ominous drifted in above the rooftops, blotting out the fiery reds and sparkling golds.

The crowd began to groan. 'Not another thunderstorm,' Jackie sighed.

Rudy and his friends knew this wasn't another thunderstorm. The dark shape might've been big enough to hide the fireworks, the stars, and even the moon, but it was far too round to be a cloud.

As the dark shape rose into the sky, the crowd below in the town square began to whisper:

'Where's the rain?'

'Shouldn't there be thunder and lightning?'

'How is that cloud moving if there's no wind?'

Another firework shot into the sky and exploded with a—

WA-BOOOMM!

As its glittering silver sparks fell like rain, the giant dark cloud split open. Instead of unleashing a downpour, it looked like the sun was somehow breaking through the darkness.

Everyone stared up, their faces filled with worried confusion.

It wasn't sunshine.

It was a large, glaring yellow eye.

The eye stared down, whipping up a storm of panic. Mr Hunter vanished in another puff of smoke, and Ms Gunther ran inside screaming. Rudy's dad was so shocked, he dropped his third plateful of sandwiches from the buffet.

As everyone else started running and screaming, Rudy, Femi, and Edie thought they should scram too. Squibly wasn't worried, though. 'It's OK,' he called out. 'That's not a monster. That's my mum!'

Every horrified face turned to Squibly.

'MUMMY!' Squibly cried, waving his tentacles.

The church chimes fell silent, and the air filled with the sound of slapping suction cups, slithering along the cobbled streets, as they pulled the huge kraken between the nearby buildings. One by one, the soggy, fleshy tentacles wormed and wriggled their way into the square.

'We're going to die!' wailed Ms Gunther as she barricaded herself inside the hall.

Before anyone could escape, the huge tentacles blocked every exit to the town square. Squibly's mum scraped past the church tower, like a giant rubbery parade balloon that had got loose!

'How is she so big?' Femi asked.

'She's an adult!' Squibly replied.

'And what are *you*?' Edie asked.

'I'm a baby!' Squibly replied.

Rudy gasped. 'How do you fit in the pond at Maplestone Park?'

'It's deeper than it looks.' Squibly shrugged and scampered on his tentacles to his mum.

Despite how odd it was to see a gigantic kraken hugging a huge one in the middle of the square, it was a lovely sight and everyone forgot their panic and smiled again.

'Where have you been?' Squibly's mum asked as her suction cups kissed him all over.

'I got washed away in the storm . . .' Squibly began. Soon he had reached the end of the story, '. . . so Rudy and his friends brought me here to help find you.'

'Thank you.' Squibly's mum smiled at Rudy, Femi, and Edie. 'I've been looking everywhere for my baby, but I would never have gone all the way through Gnarlybark Forest. Next time you visit Maplestone Park be sure to stop by.'

'Thank you, we will,' Rudy replied with a big smile.

Squibly's mum planted another kiss on his head and said, 'I'd better get you back home, your skin's beginning to dry out!'

'Of course,' Femi said. 'There's nothing worse than dry skin.'

'See you soon,' Edie said, and everyone waved them off.

'Phew, I'm glad that's all settled,' Rudy's dad said. 'I was worried they'd eat the rest of the buffet!'

'Well, luckily for you they didn't.'
Rudy's mum smiled and handed him another
plateful. 'Now, let's restart the party with
some more fireworks.'

'Absolutely!' Dad said, cramming a
sandwich in his mouth, and he hurried off.

Soon more fireworks were bursting
across the sky—

WHIZZ-BANG! FISSSSS-POP!
PUZZZARRR!

The Skeleton Ska Band started
up again too, and as everyone began
dancing in the town square, Rudy let
out a big—

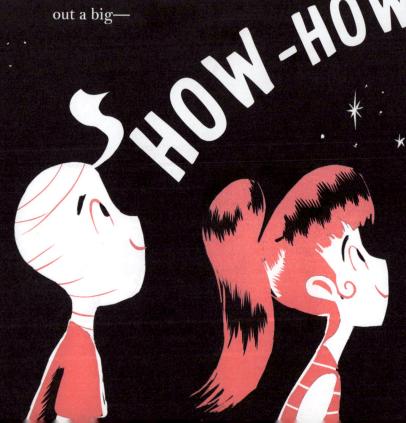

SHOW-HOW

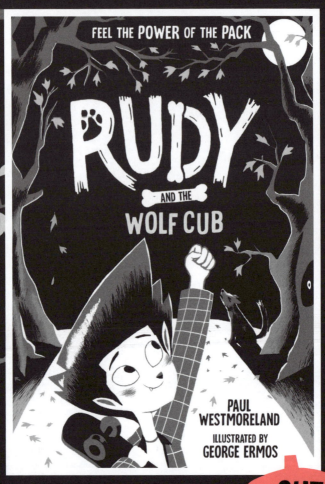

FEEL THE **POWER** OF THE PACK

RUDY
AND THE
WOLF CUB

PAUL WESTMORELAND

ILLUSTRATED BY
GEORGE ERMOS

OUT NOW

RUDY

AND THE

WOLF CUB

When Rudy finds a lost wolf cub at the skatepark, he knows he has to help him. Rudy tries everything he can think of to find the cub's pack, but they're nowhere to be seen, or smelled, and time is running out. Can a howl in the night change the fate of the little cub?

HOW-HOW-HAARROOOOWW!

RUDY

AND THE

MONSTER AT SCHOOL

There's a new boy in Rudy's school called
Frankie, and everyone says he is SCARY.
Which is really saying something, as Rudy's
class is full of ghosts and ghouls, and his
teacher is a vampire. But when Frankie gets
upset and runs away, Rudy knows he has to
help him. The trouble is, Rudy's wolf senses
lead him towards the really spooky castle
on the hill. Is Rudy brave enough to follow
his nose and find out the truth behind the
monster at school?

OUT
NOW

FEEL THE POWER OF THE PACK
RUDY
AND THE
MONSTER
AT SCHOOL
PAUL
WESTMORELAND
ILLUSTRATED BY
GEORGE ERMOS

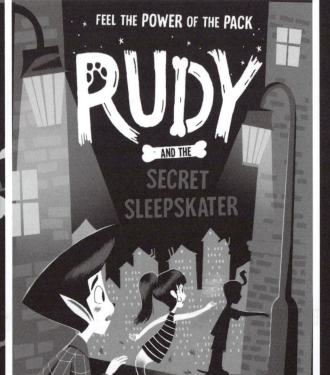

FEEL THE POWER OF THE PACK

RUDY

AND THE

SECRET SLEEPSKATER

PAUL
WESTMORELAND

ILLUSTRATED BY
GEORGE ERMOS

OUT
NOW

RUDY
AND THE
SECRET SLEEPSKATER

When Rudy and Edie go to Femi's house for a sleepover, they discover that their friend has been keeping a secret: Femi sleepwalks! And when Rudy accidentally leaves the bedroom window open he learns that not only does Femi walk in his sleep, he also skateboards in his sleep. At great speed.

Can Rudy guide Femi back to safety before everything starts to feel like a very bad dream?

HOW-HOW-HAARROOOOWW!

SKATE STARS

The Skate Stars competition has come to town, and Rudy and his friends can't wait to enter and show off their skills. But when some older wolf boys promise Rudy he'll win a gold medal if he joins their pack instead, Rudy faces a choice.

How far will Rudy go to win, and is he prepared for what he might lose . . . ?

OUT NOW

FEEL THE POWER OF THE PACK
RUDY
AND THE
SKATE STARS
PAUL WESTMORELAND
ILLUSTRATED BY
GEORGE ERMOS

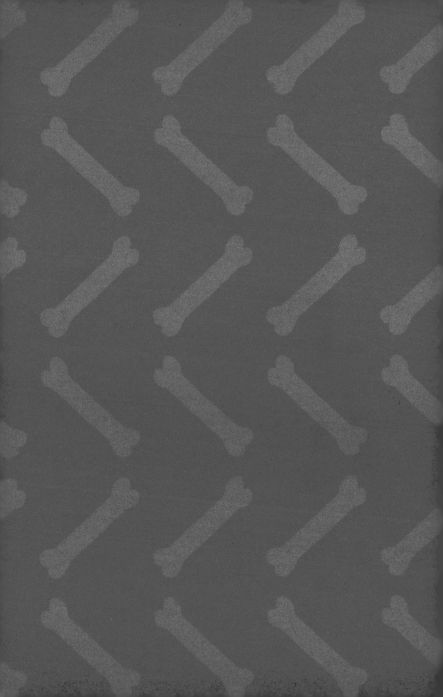

ABOUT THE
AUTHOR

I write about Rudy and his friends from a quiet room in my home, tucked away in South London. To say I love it is an understatement. It's almost as much fun as actually going on the adventures with Rudy, or hanging out with his friends at the Skateway. Although Rudy is a much better skateboarder than I am! If you love his stories, give me a

HOW-HOW-HAARROOOWW!

ABOUT THE ILLUSTRATOR

George is an illustrator, maker, and avid reader from Derbyshire. He works digitally and loves illustrating all things curious and mysterious.

LOVE RUDY?
WHY NOT TRY THESE TOO . . .